Imagine That!

PAGE PUBLISHING
Conneaut Lake, PA

First originally published by Page Publishing 2024

ISBN 979-8-89315-123-7 (pbk)
ISBN 979-8-89315-147-3 (digital)

Printed in the United States of America

Imagine That!

ALEX WRIGHT

Once upon a time, there was a little with a big imagination named Rena.

Rena lived with her mother, Alyce, and her sister, Adriana, on a tiny little street called Fourteenth Place NE in the beautiful city of Washington DC.

Rena really loved her neighborhood and all her friends. But more than that, she really loved using her wonderful imagination to pretend to be anything she wanted to be. Especially when she would watch her favorite TV commercials.

One summer day, Adriana's friends wanted her to come outside and play. Adriana yelled down the long hallway of their apartment to their mother in the kitchen to see if she could go outside and play.

Rena imagined that Adriana was going to get scolded for all that yelling in the house. Soon their mother entered the living room with a large wooden spoon with cheese on the end of it in one hand, a frown on her face, and her other hand on her hip.

Rena, however, sat with her legs crossed on the big blue checkered couch and imagined being in the Kraft macaroni and cheese commercial on TV, while Adriana ate mush for dinner as a consequence for yelling through the house.

Rena imagined Adriana's face and Adriana saying, "Oh nooo! Not mush!" Then Rena burst into laughter. After their mother finished getting on Adriana, mama left the living room to go set the table for dinner.

Rena chuckled when she saw Adriana's face upon hearing that she could not go outside to play. Adriana noticed that Rena was laughing at her.

"You're just a silly bighead, bighead!" Adriana shouted angrily.

Soon it was six o'clock on Saturday morning when Mama awakened Rena and Adriana.

"Get up, my little ladies. I was called last night to work today. I'm so sorry. I knew you both was looking forward to playing with your friends today," said Mama.

Mama felt bad that she had to work today, so she made Rena and Adriana hot pancakes in hopes of cheering them up.

"Mmmm. Hot pancakes, and with my favorite Mrs. Butterworth's syrup," said Rena.

Rena began to imagine Mrs. Butterworth talking, just like she did in the TV commercial, saying, "My syrup is thicker than the other syrups."

"I love you, Mrs. Butterworth," said Rena. She imitated the commercial just so.

"Ugh! Mrs. Butterworth can't talk to you, li'l dummy. She's just a commercial on TV!" Adriana shouted.

Rena and Adriana finished breakfast, and Mama took them to the babysitter's house. Soon the day was over, and Mama came to pick them up. On the bus ride home, Rena noticed how crowded the bus was and how different everyone looked and were dressed.

Adriana talked to Mama, who was standing nearby, about all the fun that they had at the babysitter's house that day, but Rena imagined that she was the Road Runner bird from the Bugs Bunny cartoon on TV, running amazingly fast and beating the bus home.

It was dark when the bus arrived at the corner of their street. There were no children outside playing; they had gone inside their houses for dinner. Mama made dinner too. While they were eating, Rena and Adriana told Mama about their day. Mama was happy that they enjoyed their day.

SCHOOL BUS

"May I go and watch TV? *The Carol Burnett Show* is about to start," Adriana asked with excitement.

Rena and Mama were excited too. Adriana dashed into the living room.

"I'll be right there, Adriana, as soon as I put the leftover dinner and dishes away," said Mama.

Rena sat quietly in the kitchen and imagined being a good cook like Mama.

"Hurry up! The show is starting," cried Adriana.

"Girls, it's been fun watching our favorite TV show together, but it's late, and time for your baths. How about some Mr. Bubble bubble bath?" Mama asked with a smile.

Rena immediately started to imagine that she was Mr. Bubble in the TV commercial and started to sing its jingle.

How Rena loved to watch the bubbles foam so she could pop them. Adriana loved Mr. Bubble bubble bath too; she just didn't want one right now. She wanted to stay up and watch TV a while longer.

Now that they were finished taking their bubble bath, Mama tucked them both into bed.

"Good night, girls. Sweet dreams. Love you," said Mama.

"Yelk! Bedtime," said Adriana. She lay there staring at the ceiling, but Rena fell fast asleep, dreaming about the Trix cereal commercial.

It was a beautiful sunny morning, and Mama put the girls' favorite Trix cereal and milk on the table for breakfast. When Adriana saw the Trix cereal, she was so excited until she forgot that she was upset that she had to go to bed last night. Rena was excited too.

Rena was so excited until she imagined herself being one of the kids in the Trix cereal TV commercial, saying "Silly rabbit, Trix is for kids" when the rabbit would try to eat some of the cereal.

So when Mama poured her a bowl of Trix cereal too, Rena shouted, "Silly rabbit! Trix are for kids," calling Mama a silly rabbit, just like on the TV commercial.

Rena made Mama upset when she called her a silly rabbit.

Mama knew the Trix commercial well, but she didn't expect Rena to call her a silly rabbit. "Calling names is unkind, Rena! It can hurt a person's feelings and even make them cry," said Mama. "I will not tolerate name-calling, young lady, and, Adriana! You stop that laughing, or you will not be going outside to play!" Mama said in a loud voice.

Mama sent Rena to her room for calling her a silly rabbit.

Rena did not like Mama being upset with her, and she started to cry.

Adriana followed Rena to their room. When she saw Rena crying, she stopped laughing and did not find it funny anymore that Rena had gotten into trouble with Mama. Then Adriana started to cry too.

After Mama calmed down, she came into the girls' room and explained to Rena that calling her a silly rabbit was not very funny and she must be careful about how she used her imagination. Mama then hugged Rena and Adriana, dried their tears, and told them that they may go outside to play. Mama loved Rena and Adriana very much and always wanted to do what was best for them.

Rena was glad that Mama was not upset with her anymore. Adriana stopped imagining Mama as a fire-breathing dragon too. Adriana couldn't wait to play jump rope.

Rena, however, imagined herself as being the Jolly Green Giant from the TV commercial, being taller than all the houses and apartment buildings.

"Ho! Ho! Ho! I am the Jolly Green Giant!" shouted Rena.

After a while, Mama called Rena and Adriana in for dinner. Their friends ran home for dinner too. Rena told Mama what fun she had being the Jolly Green Giant, and Adriana shared her fun about jumping rope.

"You girls may go and read while I wash the dishes, then we will have story time together. No TV tonight," said Mama.

Adriana was excited to read her favorite story, *Cinderella*. Rena liked *Goldilocks and the Three Bears* best. She imagined herself as Goldilocks and the three bears coming home and finding her sleeping in Baby Bear's bed.

Although Rena loved reading and enjoyed story time with Mama, she was a little upset that she could not watch TV tonight. Adriana started teasing her, so angrily Rena called Adriana a silly big jar head and imagined Adriana's head being a big glass jar.

Mama caught Rena calling Adriana a silly big jar head, but she did not catch Adriana teasing her sister, so Mama became upset only with Rena.

"TV can be a lot of fun, but it's not good that you watch it all the time," said Mama. "Just for calling your sister a name, Rena, you cannot watch TV for two days."

Rena tried to explain that Adriana was teasing her first, but Mama was so upset with her that she just was not listening. Rena was so upset with Mama until she went to bed without her favorite bubble bath and story time.

Adriana felt sad that she had teased Rena and gotten her into trouble, so the next morning, Adriana told Mama the truth. Mama apologized to Rena and gave her a big hug for not listening to her last night.

"I'm sorry, I did not mean to get you into trouble," said Adriana to Rena.

"I thank you for telling me the truth, but you are punished for two days with no TV or going outside to play," Mama said to Adriana.

"Now that we have settled matters, I have something wonderful to share," said Mama. "Today I am making a big family dinner. Most of your aunts, uncles, and cousins will be coming over today. Since your family is coming over, you will be allowed to watch TV and play, but just for today."

Despite being punished, Adriana was excited, and Rena was excited too.

Mama worked hard preparing all the food for the big family dinner and afterward set up the big wooden folding table that she kept in the hallway closet. The smells from the food flooded the apartment. Everything from the ham to the chocolate cake smelled and looked delicious.

Mama was happy about how well her food turned out, and she also knew how anxious Rena and Adriana would be to eat, so she reminded them that they must not touch any of the food until the family arrived, but they could have a little snack.

Rena and Adriana decided to watch TV while waiting for their cousins to come over. During the cartoon break, the Hungry Jack biscuit commercial came on. Rena started to use her imagination again.

Rena imagined the Hungry Jack biscuit giant standing outside of her window, just like he would do with the little old lady in the TV commercial.

Of course, for him to come outside of my window, I need a plate of biscuits, Rena thought to herself.

Rena remembered that Mama had made some Hungry Jack biscuits for the family dinner.

"Let me peek into the kitchen at those biscuits while Mama is still on the phone," Rena said to herself.

Rena became excited about the biscuits and started singing the jingle. "Hungry! Hungry Jack! Gobble them down, and the plate comes back for Hungry Jack!"

Adriana looked at Rena as Rena watched the Hungry Jack commercial and sang the jingle, becoming annoyed at Rena's imagination again, but this time, she did not tell Mama.

While Rena was in the kitchen, Adriana was still in their room watching TV and Mama was on the phone.

"Oh boy! Look at those delicious biscuits," said Rena to herself.

Still imagining the Hungry Jack giant coming and standing outside of her window and who always ate all the biscuits, Rena began to eat—one, two, three, four, and so on until she had eaten all twenty biscuits.

Rena looked outside of the kitchen window and was disappointed that the giant was not there. She was also sorry that she had eaten all those biscuits because now she had a stomachache.

I wonder, does the giant get a stomachache too? thought Rena.

Mama was off the phone and walked into the girls' room.

"Where's Rena?" Mama asked Adriana.

"I think she went into the kitchen after watching the Hungry Jack biscuit commercial," said Adriana.

"Oh no!" Mama shouted. Mama remembered Rena's big imagination and hoped that Rena didn't touch her biscuits.

Running to the kitchen with Adriana behind her, Mama could not believe her eyes. All her biscuits were gone, every last one of them.

"Rena! Did you eat all of my biscuits?" Mama shouted angrily.

"Yes, Mama, I'm waiting for the giant to come outside of the window since I ate all of the biscuits like he does on TV, but now my stomach hurts," replied Rena.

Mama knew that Rena has a very vivid imagination, but she never imagined that she would pull a stunt like this. "Now I have no biscuits to serve for dinner, plus you have made yourself sick, Rena!" Mama shouted.

"Go to your room right now, Rena!" Mama shouted. "You are punished until further notice, and absolutely no TV until I say so!"

Adriana was bursting with laughter, calling Rena a li'l dummy. "Why would you eat all of Mama's biscuits?" Adriana asked her.

"Stop laughing, Adriana, before you are sent to your room next!" shouted Mama. "Go into the living room, Adriana, and stay there until everyone leaves and it is time for bed!" Mama continued to shout.

Adriana wondered how long Rena would be punished, but she was not about to ask.

Finally, the family arrived, and Mama's dinner was a success despite Rena eating all the biscuits. When Mama told her sisters about what Rena had done, they laughed more hysterically than Adriana. Their laughter even made Mama chuckle a little bit.

"What am I going to do with that child?" Mama asked.

"Don't be too hard on Rena. She will outgrow it," Aunt Brenda said to Mama.

"I certainly hope so," Mama replied.

And then Aunt Brenda started to laugh again, and Mama gave another little chuckle.

After a while, all the family started to leave. Mama hugged and kissed all her sisters, brothers, nieces, and nephews, expressing how she enjoyed them and had a good time.

"Now I'm going to check on Rena and give her some more medicine for her stomach," said Mama.

Mama gave Rena some more of the pink medicine to help settle her stomach. Adriana stayed in the living room, just like Mama had told her earlier.

Mama was still upset with Rena, but not as much. Mama gave Rena a hug and said that she loved her and that she would see her in the morning. Mama also hugged Adriana and told her to get ready for bed too.

Rena decided that she did not want to imagine the Hungry Jack biscuit giant coming outside of her window anymore because he ate too many biscuits on TV and caused her to have a stomachache. Rena thought that instead of imagining so many TV commercials, she would do something better.

She would imagine the return of the first day of school. She wondered if new kids would be there this time, and if so, how many? There were only a few kids in their neighborhood who looked different from her.

Rena absolutely loved everybody and wished that she could be friends with all kids, no matter how different they looked from her.

Imagine that!

The End

About the Author

Alex Wright has a background in professions from banking to pharmacy, but she's dreamed of being an author since the age of eight. She's finally getting her wish after writing her first nonfiction children's book based on a collection of her own childhood events, titled *Imagine That!*

In addition to creative writing, Alex enjoys her dual roles of being a mother and grandmother. She also enjoys being a Christian, reading, cooking, traveling, and spending time with her family. Alex lives with her husband in Oxon Hill, Maryland. Her children and grandchildren live nearby.